Forewc

Throughout the years art, history, po
stories have shaped the way we look
communities and ourselves. This is particularly relevant when it comes to the lesbian, gay, bi-sexual and trans (LGBT) community across the globe.

Carved in stone, scribed in ink or caught on camera, the stories of our community were in existence long before the struggle for equality was even an idea.

Through the Eyes of Others confirms what has always been - that there are LGBT individuals, groups and communities who are willing to fight for what they believe is right, just and equal.

Covering the many areas of faith, nationality, sexual identity and gender identity, the pictures, photography, poems and stories reflect a snapshot of what the LGBT community (and supporters) are about. A brief timeline of LGBT history is included to give context and clarity.

Join me in celebrating the diversity of our community and ensure that our history is truly remembered and visualised.

By supporting this book the gifts of raising vital awareness and funds to various groups, charities and organisations are possible.

Sue Sanders

Nicholas Chinardet

Through the Eyes of Others came about after listening to Sue Sanders at an LGBT (Lesbian, Gay, Bisexual and Transgender) History Month event where she talked about the importance of our community reclaiming our history, recording our stories and ensuring that we pass these on to others.

I felt it was important that we do just that or we will lose important aspects of our history that may never be regained.

This got me wondering what it actually meant to be part of an 'LGBT (& Queer) Community' and how this could be portrayed to not only show the differences that exist within our community, yet also to show that many individuals support us who do not necessary identify as LGBT or Q and stand with us in ensuring we have equal rights and are recognised in society.

Over 30 individuals voluntarily contributed their time to ensure ***Through the Eyes of Others*** came to fruition.

We felt it was important that these books also raise funds and awareness for various charities, groups and organisations.

I hope you enjoy ***Through the Eyes of Others*** and that you'll encourage others to purchase copies, reclaim our history and share the stories, images, artwork with many others – whilst continuing to support future editions over the next few years.

Thank you.

Robert J Brown

David Miles

Upon being told that a male backbench MP had been caught by the press performing indecent acts with a guardsman in St James' Park during one of the coldest February nights in 30 years, Sir Winston Churchill replied:

"Makes you proud to be British doesn't it?"

Stephan Gregoire

GoDPhotography

PRIDE

If I wanted
to be thinner
I'd skip dinner
shackle
my limbs
to a treadmill

If I wanted
to be bigger
a weightlifter
I'd lift cars
pull bars
and fight

If I wanted
your approval
I'd demand it
never ask
always
assured

If I wanted
to be patronised
I'd be quiet
or beg
on all fours

Instead I stand here
resilient
complete
and brush the droplets
of your disapproval
from my back

Adam Lowe

Orthodox Love

Lesvos, Mykonos, Athens and various other Greek cities have been havens for the LGBT community for centuries.

Why is Greece such a magnet for same sex couples? History speaks for itself.

Considered by many to be the "***cradle of homosexuality***," as well as the birthplace of democracy, philosophy, and many modern sciences, Greece is a nation that takes great pride in its ancient roots.

However, modern Greece is a largely conservative society, strongly influenced by the dominant Greek Orthodox church and Mediterranean notions of "machismo."

Although there is a certain acceptance of homoerotic love, there is little tolerance in the Greek mainstream for openly queer lifestyles.

Gay, lesbian, bisexual, and transgender activists have worked since the 1970s to increase queer visibility and improve the status of gay men and lesbians in Greek society.

Some Greek islands, notably Mikonos for men and Lesvos for women, have become gay tourist destinations, drawing thousands of international queers every year and giving Greek gays and lesbians a chance to be themselves in public.

Lesvos, the island on which Sappho lived, has Skala Eressos, the town where Sappho was born and attracts European lesbians in great numbers and although queer lifestyles are largely closeted in the countryside, most large cites, such as Athens, Iraklion, and Thessaloniki have gay and lesbian bars.

In societies where masculinity is revered, homoerotic feelings between men are often understood and tacitly accepted, as long as heterosexual lifestyles are maintained. Lesbians, however, as women who do not need men, are often almost inconceivable in such cultures.

Lesbian visibility continues to be a problem in Greek society, and courageous activists such as Maria Catsicadacou and Christiana Lambrinidis have worked in different ways to give Greek dykes a public face.

Catsicadacou, who also uses the name Maria Cyberdyke, has worked on lesbian radio shows and has been central in organizing large queer parties, both in Athens and in the lesbian resort town of Skala Eressos on the island of Lesvos.

Whilst a valued member of the European Union, Greece has flatly rebuffed the European Parliament's call in 2000 for member states to recognise gay and lesbian unions. Whilst Greece is considered the 'cradle of homosexuality, the Greek Orthodox Church condemns all expressions of personal sexual experience which prove contrary to the definite and unalterable function ascribed to sex by God's ordinance and expressed in man's experience as a law of nature.

The Orthodox Church cannot subscribe to the demand that homosexuals be recognized by society and its agencies as legal spouses and as deserving the same respect as men and women enjoy in the state of wedlock.

With the most recent rise of various right-wing groups, supported by some of Greece's MPs, the situation for those from the LGBT community is getting worse, not better, yet hope still shines in the spirit of those of us still fighting for equality, freedom and the right to love who we wish.

anonymous

My sex is my voice and my voice is muted

It has become hoarse and distorted frustrated disturbed

I want to shout with joy for the love of my sex

But I scream into a tunnel I can barely hear myself

My sex is not my life it is a part of my life

That has been made bigger by the hate and fear of others

I don't want to yell at you or expose myself to your hatred

But because of my sex and love of my sex I have that role

I have to put myself and my sex in front of you in the headlines

To be jeered and bullied

I don't want to go there but in your eyes my sex dictates

I cannot stand by my lover and hold his hand in a busy street

And kiss his lips under blue skies

You take your lover by the hand and fear nothing

While we kiss in dark alleys one eye behind us

Never totally relaxed not even in our beds in our home

Think about that.

Nicolas Collins

I wrote this poem many years ago as a response to Clause 28 - I was out demonstrating in Liverpool and Manchester to change this appalling bill - successfully in the end. However - it seems to be too relevant today again with the news from St Petersburg in Russia – this in solidarity with all gay people across the world fighting for equality and love.

Nicolas Collins

African, Black and Gay

I am asked. You are at, or have passed the marrying age so what are you doing? “What do you think of the daughter of ‘our friend’?

These and other questions and the endless tricks to get me to date girls, without seeking any consent, is a constant fact of my and many other Somali gay men's life.

There are diverse cultures around the world, and these are usually formed through shared customs, languages and beliefs.

Cultures are important to human society because they help them to form people’s identities, so that they could make sense of their lives and the world that is around them. Culture cannot be entirely bad, they give people a sense of belonging and pride.

What needs acknowledgement is the fact that all cultures have negative aspects in them, and that, if not corrected by the knowledge humans acquire from understanding the world or peoples’ lives those bad aspects could oppress or cause serious psychological damage to sizeable sections of society.

The catalyst for many Somali leaving their homeland was the ugly civil war and in the UK we found a new home with the wonder of being able to have the opportunity to experience and learn about cultures that are different to our own.

This allows us to make comparisons and increase our knowledge about the increased awareness of our own culture and therefore should help us abolish all forms of discrimination against various members of our community.

However it appears that many Somali haven’t taken advantage of the situation, because many ignore and bury their heads in the sand when confronted with the realities in their adopted country.

There are a number of reasons as to why someone doesn't conform to the expectation of marriage: the first and easiest one is even though a person wants to get married, they don't meet the right person – that doesn't mean that the don't engage in 'forbidden' sexual practices. They may simply not be interested in sex or they may just not be interested in getting married and of course, like me, they may just be LGB or T.

The reason why I haven't got married is because I am gay. I like men. There, we have it . . . a black gay East African Somali – out and proud!

Just because someone isn't married, that doesn't mean that they are gay – they are just being how they are and may not want to be labelled and I know many happy Somali in loving relationships who are not gay and are not married.

I also know many gays who conform to demands in society and get married and have children whilst knowing that they are gay.

I have made the decision to be honest about my life and sexuality and whilst it hasn't been easy, I started the Somali Gay Community to help and support others like me to find solace and to confront and fight against all forms of discrimination in our community.

We need to show that the wider Somali community are not all unforgiving, hostile or intolerant.

Murad

African, White and Gay

Apartheid is awful. Discrimination of any kind is horrendous.

Many of us within the white, gay African community felt safe within our homes. We were able to openly go to bars and clubs, meet with each other, have lovers of other races. That has all changed in many countries across our beautiful continent.

I won't say exactly what country I am from in Africa, however we all know that Zimbabwe, South Africa, Uganda, Ghana, Nigeria and other countries across Africa are ensuring that equality does not mean equality.

We have despot leaders in Zimbabwe saying that all LGBT people are "worse than dogs".

We have youth leaders of the African National Congress (ANC) in South Africa singing that whites should be shot.

We have religious leaders in Uganda trying to ensure that any rights given to others are not allowed to those from within the LGBT community!

We have the head of the Catholic Church and the head of the Anglican Church speaking together against equality for members of the LGBT community and being supported by other congregations, other religious communities, other human beings!

Out of 54 sovereign states in the continent of Africa only 14 have male to male sexual activity as legal, with only 22 having female to female sexual activity as legal – whist Nigeria has male to male sexual activity as illegal and female to female sexual activity legal only in some areas of the country.

You would have thought that many of these 'Commonwealth' countries, whom have accepted Queen Elizabeth II as head of state, would have also ensured that many of their own queens would be protected – unfortunately that is not the case!

Why can't I be equal in my own country?

When in Zambia I was exorcised by ministers of the Kingdom Hall of Jehovah. I was told that I was evil, that I was not of this earth – but if GOD made me in his image, am I not just like him?

There are six admonitions in the bible towards homosexuals. There are **362** admonitions against heterosexuals in the same bible.

That does not mean GOD hates heterosexuals - it simply means that they need more supervision.

If I am to follow my heart **and** the bible, does that also then mean I am not to eat shellfish? Am I not allowed to wear woven cloth or mixed threads?

I came to the UK to be safe, secure in the knowledge that I can be free to be who I am, yet how safe am I?

I have been told many times to go back to 'my country' – what is my country? How can I go back to a country that doesn't want me to exist, doesn't want me to be who I am?

I pray that I can live my life in the UK so that I can be open and love the person I am with, yet I am fearful that I will not be allowed to stay.

Do people not understand how hard it is to be openly gay, Christian and White in Africa?

Godfrey

Our History Remembered

Many of us have heard of The Stonewall Riots – a time in Lesbian, Gay, Bi-sexual and Trans (LGBT) History which defined the LGBT movement as a pivotal point in the start of gaining equality and rights in society.

The Stonewall Inn played a significant part in the modern gay rights movement from the late 1960s. The team running the inn experienced several police raids for varying reasons from claims of vice to allegations of trading alcohol without appropriate licenses.

After becoming continually frustrated with these raids the Stonewall Inn Riots began on 27 June 1969 when New York City police officers raided the bar. The resulting riots lasted three days, eventually changing the modern gay rights situation on a worldwide basis.

However, there have been LGBT people around for centuries – how do we know? Just look at the resultant timeline:

Around 10th millennium BC – mankind started to make artefacts which suggest an appreciation of homosexual eroticism. Some examples can be found in caves and other buildings as well as many phallic statues along with evidence of female masturbation found at Gorge d'Enfere in France.

25 / 25th Century BC – Khnumhotep and Niankhkhumn's tomb in Egypt. The relationship between the two is unknown, however homosexuality was known to have been practised.

7th Century BC – marriage between men was not legally recognised, although life-long relationships between adult men were not uncommon. Sappho of Lesvos writes her famous love poems to young women, providing the eventual inspiration for the word lesbian.

6th Century BC – The Roman Republic was found with homosexuality widespread and legalised throughout the republic.

4th Century BC – Plato's 'Symposium' is published which argues that love between males is the highest form and that sex with women (by men) is lustful and is only use for reproduction.

4th Century – the first law against same sex marriage was promulgated by the Christian emperors Constantius II and Constans. Nearly 50 years later in 390AD the Christian emperors Valentinian II, Theodosius I and Arcadius declared homosexual sex to be illegal and those who were guilty of it were condemned to be burned alive in front of public audiences.

11th Century – in Scandinavia the cult of transvestism persists for centuries.

12th Century – the Council of London took measures to ensure that the English public knew that homosexuality was sinful.

13th Century – Homosexual activity radically passes from being completely legal in most of Europe to incurring the death penalty in many countries.

In France, if you were found to have engaged in same sexual activity, on the first offence you lost your testicles, the second your 'member' and on the third you were burnt.

Women who were caught engaging in same sexual activity were often mutilated and executed.

14th Century – Jan van Aersdone and Willem Case were executed in Antwerp for engaging in 'gay sex'. One other couple whose names have stood the sands of time to this day are Giovanni Braganza and Nicoleto Marmagna of Venice.

John Ryheker was on of the first known transvestites who work in London and Oxford as a 'prostitute'. He was arrested in 1395 for cross-dressing.

15th Century – Leonardo da Vinci and others were charged with sodomy . . . and acquitted! In Spain during 1483 the inquisition began and sodomites (those who engaged in same sexual activity) were stoned, castrated and burned – over 1,500 people were prosecuted between 1540 and 1700.

16th Century – King Henry VII passes the Buggery Act 1533 making all male same sexual activity punishable by death. Mary Tudor removes all laws passed by Henry VIII when she ascended the throne in 1553. Elizabeth I reinstates the sodomy laws when she ascended the throne in 1558.

17th Century – in 1649 Sarah White Norman was the first known conviction for 'lesbian activity' in Plymouth, North America. She was charged with "Lewd behaviour each with other upon a bed" – her partner Mary Vincent Hammon was not charged with an offence as she was under 16 years old.

Sina Sparrow

Saffy's (Saffron) World

What can I say? I have two of everything and only one heart and one mind. I like two of everything. I also have one room where I get to be me – so the room and me makes two actually.

Being born in Liverpool there is two of everything: two cathedrals, two football teams, two liver birds and I've now also got two choices in one complex sexuality – I am not a lesbian, nor am I heterosexual. I am not into labels – only men **and** women, and of course I am in to me (does that make three?).

I am from two cultures from two continents: African (Sierra Leone) and European (UK) – yet there is whole lot more to me than others may realize; I am from a two-religion home: Muslim and Christian. However, I choose Buddhism – Nichiren Daishonin's Buddhism to be exact.

In Nichiren Daishonin's Buddhism I find that we do everything in two: mentor and disciple relationship; our daily prayers are done twice a day and good and evil are two concepts in one. So you could say I love the bi concept of two.

When loving a man I love to embrace his femininity as well as him. When loving a woman I embrace her masculinity as well as her. They always overlap.

I find that some straight women treat me like a straight man and some gay men treat me like a man. Bisexual women, well, we get along fine – until there is a woman we both want to be with – yet isn't that the case with most friends?

Liverpool heavily breathes heterosexuality and I remember one time being battered for wearing pants as no "African" ever wore trousers. I remember playing football with the lads after school and would strip tease with girls and show each other our tits.

Fascinated by the kissing competitions amongst the girls you were classed either as a lesbian or heterosexual – that's just how it seemed to be in 'The Pool' in those days.

At West African parties I attended and looked forward to, how the butt slapping, the dragging on the dance floor (by the women more so than the men) would happen all the time. The Ghanians, Gambians, Sierra Leonians, Nigerians, Mali, Senegalese, how they would encourage you to shake ya ting.

Experiences at work varied as they were not used to having a 'bi-woman' around. At Pride I was given 'lesbian leaflets', yet why no 'bi leaflets'? At African parties I was told that I could not love another woman – yet I still love men as well – what is wrong with that? When clubbing it gets even more interesting as I have the whole room to chose from and not just half of it. Yet choosing whether to go to a straight club or a lesbian / gay club can be the issue – not whom I fancy. Where are the bi clubs, then I wouldn't need to 'come out' every time I 'go out'!

Practising Nichiren Buddhism has been a benefit for me. Going to an LGBT meeting in Soho 10 years ago I wasn't asked what sexuality I was, I was welcomed and made to feel comfortable when I eventually did introduce myself as a sexually aware bi-sexual Afro-Euro woman.

Meeting other bi-woman was wonderful and gave me affirmation as to the fact that we are many and we are varied.

Many may not understand what bi individuals have to go through, yet we have always been here and like our fellow LGT individuals, we will also be here. Our History is everyone's history. I know who I am!

Saffy

anonymous

FRUIT

You call me a fruit,
and I agree,
say

a fruit is ripe,
promising seeds,
bursting with juice.

You call me a fruit,
as though a vegetable
while I recite a litany
of fresh attributes:

a fruit is rich,
remembers its roots,
nourishes, quenches,
makes a display of any table.

I say, I am the apple
that announces the gravity
of a given situation;
I am the pomegranate
whose gemstones teach
of the burden of possession;
I am the fig
our ancestors couldn't resist.

You call me a fruit
and I agree:
soft, round and sweet.
Peel back my layers,
take a look at my pips.
Full as a melon,
sharp as a lime,
come over here
and bite me.

Adam Lowe

Ellis Collins

Our History Remembered

18th Century – In Germany, Catherina Margaretha Linck is executed for sodomy in 1721.

In 1726 three men are executed after Mother Cap's molly house in London is raided by police. In 1785 Jeremy Bentham (1748-1832) is one of the first people to argue for the decriminalisation of sodomy in England.

In 1791 France and Andorra become the first countries in Europe to decriminalise same sex acts between consenting adults.

19th Century – during the 19th Century many countries across the world decriminalised homosexual / same sex acts including:

- Netherlands (1811)
- Indonesia (1811)
- Brazil (1830)
- Portugal (1852)
- The Ottoman Empire (predecessor of Turkey – 1858)
- San Marino (1865)
- Guatemala (1871)
- Mexico (1871)
- Empire of Japan (1880)
- Argentina (1886)

The last known execution for homosexuality in Great Britain was in 1836.

For the first time in history, homosexuality becomes illegal in Poland in 1835 after the occupying Russian Empire imposed repressive laws. The German Empire criminalises homosexuality in 1871.

In 1867, Karl Heinrich Ulrichs became the first known self-proclaimed homosexual and spoke out for equal rights. The term homosexual first appeared in print in 1869.

The first homosexual rights groups are formed in 1897 – one is called the Scientific Humanitarian Committee, the other the Order of Chaeronea.

20th Century – New York Police Department raided a gay bathhouse in 1903; the first ever recorded incident.

In 1913, the word 'faggot' is first used in print with regards to referencing gays. The wording of this was:

"All the fagots [sic] (sissies) will be dressed in drag tonight"

The actual word 'gay', referring to homosexuals, was not used until 1920. In 1921 in England there was an attempt to make lesbianism illegal – luckily it failed.

In 1917, during the October Revolution, Russia repeals the previous criminal code in its entirety – this was then officially decriminalised again in 1922.

In 1928, The Well of Loneliness by Radclyffe Hall was published; this book was (and continues to be) a source of inspiration to lesbians all over the world.

In 1961, the Vatican declares that:

“anyone who is affected by the perverse inclination towards homosexuality should not be allowed to take religious vows or be ordained within the Roman Catholic Church”

Countries and territories that decriminalised homosexuality / same-sex acts from the early 1900’s up to early 1970’s include:

- Panama (1924)
- Paraguay (1924)
- Peru (1924)
- Demark (1933)
- Philippines (1933)
- Uruguay (1934)
- Iceland (1940)
- Switzerland (1942)
- Sweden (1944)
- Suriname (1944)
- Portugal (1945 – for the second time)
- Czechoslovakia (1961)
- Hungary (1961)
- England (1967)
- Illinois, USA (1967)
- Wales (1967)
- East Germany (1968)
- Bulgaria (1968)
- Canada (1969)
- Costa Rica (1971)
- Finland (1971)
- Austria (1971)
- Colorado, USA (1971)
- Oregon, USA (1971)
- Hawaii, USA (1972)
- Norway (1972)

Wisdom

Like a jeweller's masterpiece,

Wisdom is displayed

Proving that over time

It improves with age

Precious and valuable

And afforded by few.

A companion on the clever

A friend of the shrewd.

It's enduring and is used

As a foundation for knowledge
An essential doctrine
At the most exclusive college.
But Hark! It's substance can
Only be absorbed
By the most open minds
Not the idle or bored.
The smoothness of its surface
Is appreciated by those,
Who recognise that without it
Their lives would be morose.
Like the most ancient stones
Wisdom has been here
And its structure becomes more honed
Year after year.
If used carefully in our lives
We ensure success and contentment
And surely that is what we each
Should aspire to in fulfilment?
So respect and admire
The potential of wisdom
As life without it
Would be worthless, full of boredom.

Charlotte Adejayan *(photography) /* ***Colette Dathorne*** *(poem)*

Celtic Buddhist

To have a mixed heritage can at times be a blessing in disguise.

Not knowing which team to support, which faith to believe in or which country to say you're from . . . therefore, I like to say that I am a global citizen, having English, Irish and Scottish heritage within my family.

My dad was an army Sergeant and at a young age I witnessed the horrors and effects war can have on a family, a society and the world at large.

Based around Essex, living in Ipswich and with family members in the area, at the age of seven we moved up to Tayside away from Suffolk – though I am not sure of the exact reasons why.

Having an East Anglian accent meant I stood out from the rest of the primary school children and as such was bullied and made to go to elocution lessons to 'speak properly' and rrrrrrroll my 'r's.

After moving to London at the age of 17 years old, I started working full time from the age of 18 years old and was lucky enough to meet the Buddhism of Nichiren Daishonin at quite an early age.

Attending my first SGI Buddhist discussion meeting in Angel, Islington (London) and seeing people I recognised from the gay and lesbian bars and clubs I decided that chanting 'nam myoho renge kyo' was the right thing for me.

Chanting brings the entirety of the universe together and brings all aspects of my heritage, my culture, my belief system and my being in to one and enables me to support myself and others to the best of my ability and as society dictates.

Gaining strength from historical figures such as Winston Churchill, Florence Nightingale, Rosa Parks, Gandhi, Martin Luther King, Daisaku Ikeda and Nichiren Daishonin, along with others including the Maori people of Parihaka I feel that as long as I continue to chant and speak out where I see injustice, I can continue to move forward and hopefully inspire others to move forward as well – whatever their faith, belief, religion, colour, creed, sexuality or gender identity.

Being a 'Celtic Buddhist' is more than just understanding where I am from and what I want to achieve with my life, it's about seeing how and where I can fit in and support others to do the same.

I do the things I do because I want to, not because I have to.

In Soka Gakkai International (SGI) we have a 'president' and we have 'general directors' of our worldwide organisations. There are many celebrities who chant 'nam myoho renge kyo', yet in Nichiren Buddhism (even within SGI) we have no 'spiritual leader' as such.

Each and every one of us are taught that we are a Buddha and as Daisaku Ikeda says, each of us are 'Presidents of Soka Gakkai International . . . ennobled with the courage of a lion and the heart of a queen.

First and foremost though we are all human beings and for those of us who chant the Daimoku as the Lotus Sutra teaches us, we can reveal the Buddhahood from within ourselves.

We can create value just as the Lotus Sutra teaches. We can hopefully inspire others to do more for others and do more for their community and themselves – that, for me, is what it is all about.

Robert J Brown

Richard Hoey

I was born in 1960
I was born illegal
In 1967 I was partially decriminalised
In the 70s I was the butt of middle-aged men's TV jokes
I was limp wristed and weak
Yet I was so dangerous
That you had to turn your backs to the wall
If I walked into the room

In the 80s I may have had AIDS
And I was toxic
I was a danger to your children
So in 1988 I was made unspeakable

In 1994 I was partially re-decriminalised
Or is it re-partially decriminalised?
In 2000 I was decriminalised and
I could call myself a woman if I wanted

In 2003 I became mentionable again and
You couldn't sack me just for being gay

In 2005 I could celebrate my relationship
And soon I'll be able to marry –
But not in a church

I don't expect you all to love me
But if you hate me so much that
You attack me the law –
The law that protected you for centuries
Will now protect me

Is it all right now?
Some people still laugh at me on TV
Some people say I'll go to Hell
A few people want to put me there personally

But it's been a hell of a half-century
I think you'll agree

Tony Fenwick

Bi-Tween the Sheets

Are you gay, lesbian or questioning? What if you are neither and are not sure where you fit in today's labelled environment? Labels are for clothes. What does it mean to be bisexual?

In the past is has been reported by many within the LGBT community that bisexual women are doing a disservice to the lesbian community – why and how is that? Bisexual women are just that, bi-sexual; we are neither lesbian nor straight.

Surveys and statics from our community show that it's actually harder for someone to come out as 'bi' as it is to come out as LG or T due to many preconceived misconceptions.

I happen to be bisexual. Am I denying my gayness? Not at all. Am I denying my hettiness? Not at all. I just happen to be sexually aroused by both men and women, yet that doesn't meant that I am turned on by ALL men and ALL women.

Bisexuals are often not understood in many communities as some small minded people think that we're just in it for the sex: 'greedy' or 'the best of both worlds' is a phrase often cited, yet we can't help it if we are attracted to both men and women.

Personally I go for the soul.

If I am attracted to a person by the way they are, then the physical appearance is secondary. That doesn't mean to say that I'm not attracted to looks – it just means that I don't use that as my 'guiding principle' when determining who I want to date, sleep or settle down with.

And yes, bisexual people can have very good monogamous relationships.

If you are male or female in the 'gay scene' and your friends find out that you've suddenly met someone of the opposite sex you can often be vilified, ostracized and accused of 'selling out'. You are often told that you are no longer part of the LGBT community as you have an opposite sex partner and are only interested in 'conforming' to the social norms.

If I **was** interested in conforming, then I certainly wouldn't choose to be bisexual.

Just as no-one can determine what colour of eyes they have, or the colour of skin they have (unless they either bleach or tan) most people also cannot determine what sexuality (or gender identity) they have.

At a recent conference I attended some people seemed to love the fact that there was more than one bisexual in the room. It amazed me as I didn't realise we were on show for the rest of the conference to look and point at. I didn't realise, as a human being, that my bits were different than anybody else's.

The bi-sexual people I know are not scared to 'come out', they're just upset at not being listened to or understood.

Yes we are attracted to both sexes, yet if we meet someone, regardless of what gender that person is, what we want is a loving, stable relationship.

If that happens to be female (for me) then I'm a lesbian. If male, then I'm straight. Where's the problem?

Love is Love regardless of gender.

anonymous

Eve Poland

Look at Me

Look at me,
Look at me and remember,
Look at my face and hear my voice....
Because whatever you think,
this is my place too
And I will not be forgotten.
However many blocks you place in my way, I will overcome.
However many challenges I have to rise to,
I will not lay down to you
Or your kind.

I can dream and I will dream
I will be part of the world's future.
Don't call me by your label
Because I'm not.
Don't tell me to look in the mirror
And see the face you want me to see, and tell me to recognise
An unfamiliar place.
I have a map and I have a home.
I will be defiant
I will have my land
My name is on the paper
And that is my truth.

I will be better, stronger, greater
Than anything or anyone you can imagine.
I will be the beauty of the butterfly.
I am trans, hear the beat
Of my wings.
Now I know there's
Peace in self discovery...
And I can now hear the music:
My band and my people,
Playing the music I can march to.
And the tears on my cheeks
Will wash away yesterday.

Victoria Candos

Hellz Bellz

Her Majesty's Prison Service

A hidden sacrifice,

To many,

The lowest of the low.

Yet to those who know,

Satisfaction guaranteed.

A job done well,

A job no-one talks about,

Memories of those whom have gone before.

A history of dedication and sacrifice,

Her Majesty's hidden service.

anonymous

Beyond the Veil

When I wear the niqab I am safe.

When I walk down the street I feel warm and secure – solid in my faith and in my love.

I wear the niqab so that I can be free to be myself – a woman who enjoys the love and company of other women. For women like me in my community, I wear the niqab as it symbolises my personal choice and my personal faith – it is part of who I am – whether I chose to wear it or not is my choice.

Why? Because I feel free inside. I feel the flowing air happy and feel wonderfully enlightened, a bit like wearing a kilt for the Scottish or a habit for the nun. That is why I wear mine – for the freedom.

We initially met during prayers one sunny Friday afternoon in Dhaka. The wind moved her niqab lightly across her body as she knelt down to pray.

She looked over towards me with her brown eyes and intensely looked at me. It struck me, those eyes, everything is said in the eyes. The pain, the horror, the fear, the love. When I looked in to her eyes I saw love.

Her eyes lit up the room when she came in, we were both younger then and already married, yet something about her tugged at my heart; a loving, a knowing, a yearning.

The next time we met was over 20 years later during prayers in East London. I instantly recognised those eyes and she also recognised and felt me deep inside her heart. I saw the pain, the years of abuse, of work, of love and of caring. I wanted her love.

We studied English together and began to spend more and more time in each other's company, learning about our new life, our new society and ourselves. As we were reading her hand gently touched mine, we grew to a gentle lingering caress.

It took us a few more months before we started to understand and recognise what was happening and whilst not fully conscious of it happening, we removed our niqab and saw each other in full spendour.

At first I felt a tingly feeling as if I had been stung by nettles, then she gently squeezed my hand as she looked in to my eyes.

Those eyes – that is why we wear the niqab – the eyes go directly in to the heart. We feel safe when wearing the niqab as no-one can see who we really are – except ourselves.

When we are by ourselves, without the men, we can take off our niqab and be together again.

Fun, love, laughter and at ease. At ease with each other and that is how we fell in love. How can two Muslim women fall in love I hear you ask – quite simple really – we just did.

I love her. She loves me. No questions asked, no answers needed. It just is.

There are those who do not like our love, so we have to hide our true feelings beyond our veils and show our love to each other throw our eyes. When we have our time together alone, that is our precious time, our quiet time.

Though our neighbours wouldn't think that we were quiet by the noise that we make. Our husbands at work, our children at school – we then have time to explore, to understand, to love.

anonymous

Alison Baskerville

The Captured Hermaphrodite : The Pansy

XXXona

The Third Gender

The Vedic literature is supreme, and unsurprisingly it offers a very deep understanding of gender categories and sexual orientation.

A verse from the Srimad Bhagavatam states that there are three states of gender identity: female, male and "none of both" (nobhayam), which Srila Prabhupada translated as "neutral eunuch."

maya hy esa maya srista
yat pumamsam striyam satim
manyase nobhayam yad vai
hamsau pasyavayor gatim

"Sometimes you think yourself a man, sometimes a chaste woman and sometimes a neutral eunuch. This is all because of the body, which is created by the illusory energy. This illusory energy is My potency, and actually both of us – you and I – are pure spiritual identities. I am trying to explain the position of our faith." (*Bhag. 4.28.61*).

In other places Srila Prabhupada refers to the latter group as the "in-between" gender (e.g. *Srimad Bhagavatam 10.1, notes).*

Various Vedic scriptures including Puranas, medical and astrological texts lay out the Vedic gender approach, clearly accepting a third-gender category. Specific definitions can be found in the Caraka Samhita (*4.2, a Vedic medical text*); Sushruta Samhita (*3.2, a Vedic medical text*); Narada-smriti (*12.8-18, Dharma Shastra*); Kamatantra (*Kama Shastra*); and Smriti-Ratnavali (*a medieval Dharma Shastra summary*), as well as in various Sanskrit dictionaries and lexicons such as the Amarakosa and Sabda-Kalpa-Druma.
Therein references are made to "eunuchs" as "tritiya prakriti", a

category that actually comprises all those persons that are physically and/or mentally not exclusively defined as male or female. This means that bisexual, homosexual, intersexual, transsexual and asexual persons are part of this third gender.

Many of the Dharma Shastra texts like Manusmriti, Narada-smriti, Yajnavalkya-smriti and the four major Dharmasutras state that the third gender should be at least minimally maintained by their family members since they do not (*generally*) have children (*Manusmriti 9.202).* The Artha Shastra also confirms this (*3.5.30-32*). The Vasistha Dharmasutra further mentions that the king should maintain third-gender citizens with no family members (*19.35-36*). The Artha Shastra also prohibits the vilification of third-gender men or women (*3.18.4-5).* Besides these references, there is the example of Maharaja Virata protecting Brihannala as a guest in his city.

It can be argued that Vedic scriptures accept the third sex as a constant part of human society, requiring and deserving protection instead of exclusion and discrimination with Vedic society offering special protection to this group and established specific city districts for third-gendered people, amongst other protections. Suitable jobs were also specifically reserved for them in conjunction with a set of rules.

According to Vedic astrology, an individual's charts would point to third-gendered persons having spiritual talents, and therefore, third-gendered children were often trained to live as lifelong celibates and to assume the role of priests later on.

Entangled in material activities, they are considered semi-saintly, which makes their blessings and curses especially respected.

Galva108

Top - Respect / Middle - Ambition / Bottom - Passion

Joel Cable

As I Let You Go

The Little Girl inside me is lost forever,
Tortured by your brutality and cruel comments together.

Dreams of a blissful union are shattered abruptly,
Your infidelity and forbidden fatherhood destroying me completely.

Promises of utter faithfulness are betrayed instantly,
Your phone pictures and texts exposing you vividly.

The vodka inside me is soothing me gently.
As I focus on each offence less intently.

But tomorrow to Rehab I submit myself,
In a desperate measure to regain my health.

As my addiction to you is resolved so slow,
I shall bid you Goodbye as I let you go.

Charlotte Adejayan *(photography) /* ***Colette Dathorne*** *(poem)*

Same Mind, Different Body

Wherever I went I was asked 'what' I was.

Not who I was or what my name was, simply "What are you?"

Do I not look like a human being? I know who and what I am, so is it really any business of yours?

To share, I was genetically born female and at birth was registered as such, yet as I grew up I knew that I felt and was male: I just didn't have the 'correct' genitalia. When I first realised that there was such a term as 'TransMan' I instantly knew that that was what society would pigeon hole me as.

Finding others like me was more difficult. I would go out in to the lesbian and gay bars and clubs yet felt somehow different and not accepted. I was a man in a woman's body and attracted to woman – was I straight or should I simply try and be a lesbian?

Others are still not able to get their heads around it – even within the lesbian, gay and bi-sexual (LGB) community. I am not asking others to fully understand, simply to accept me for my choices and to accept me as a contributing member of society.

Do we go to other human beings and ask to see their 'meat and two veg' to prove their gender identity? Do we ask others about their personal sexual history and how 'we' do it?

Do others not have enough entertainment or issues in their own life without creating situations that are of no consequence to them? Is your life not stimulating enough for you to live it?

When I started to dress as a man no-one questioned it due to the fact that I already looked quite masculine.

Many thought I was a 'butch dyke'. I am not, I am a man trapped in a woman's body.

My gender identity changes and at times so does my sexuality. When I was female identified and with a woman I was a lesbian – now that I am male identified and with a woman I am straight. That's the reality of the situation.

I have always known that I was 'different' from the mainstream, yet what does it mean to be 'different'? just because I am not like you, does not mean you have to then judge me – if you don't fully understand, then ask. Even if you don't understand, just accept me as a human being.

Then the real challenges started to appear:

- Who and where do I go for support?
- Where do I go for surgery if I want it?
- How do I find others like me?
- How can I afford all the treatments?
- What about issues such as my birth certificate, passport?
- How do I choose my own name?

In the UK there are now many laws which support and protect those from the 'trans community'. Laws which offer some forms of protection from discrimination – yet, this wasn't always the case and still many issues of discrimination still exist.

I and many others have been sacked and vilified simply for wanting to feel safe and secure within myself and be true to who I am in today's society – and there are many of us.

We exist in many different guises and professions. We are in loving and stable relationships. We are happy and our true to ourselves and we contribute to society as a whole.

anonymous

Easter for Gays

Easter is a period of lamentation for the followers of Jesus Christ (Christians) with many Lesbians, Gays, Bisexuals, Transgender and Intersex (LGBTI) people identifying with the suffering of the risen Lord.

The time that Jesus the saviour of the world was faced with his own mortality, he was rejected, insulted and despised by those who he came to save. This is often the daily life of many LGBTI people around the world today. Ostracised and disregarded by our primary faith communities, we live daily in fear of family, friends and State.

The beginning of Lent (Ash Wednesday) marked the run up to the arrest, trial, and death and finally the resurrection of Jesus Christ. He suffered tremendous pains in his effort to share the good news of freedom and liberation, to release the captives and let the oppressed go free (Luke 4:18).

The message of Christ is still echoed around the world and more so by many inclusive and affirming ministries, such as House Of Rainbow Fellowship and the Metropolitan Community Church.

They exist to remind LGBTI people that they too can share in the good news of redemption and salvation, be able to renew their Christian faith through baptism, reconciliation and spirituality.

Christ died for all people and in the season of Lent we remember Jesus, we remember him through his words and ministry of inclusion, through the feast of the Passover, his broken body and blood pour out for all.

The death of Jesus is not a favour for one group of people, but an act of liberation for all people and more so for LGBTI people.

I can only share in the hope that many will accept Christ as saviour and understand that we are wonderfully and fearfully made in the image of God.

For LGBTI people, it is important that we make a connection at Eastertime of our full understanding of the reason for the season, a solemn and joyful remembrance of liberation. When Jesus hung on the tree and died, he took away our sins, pain and anxiety, this act of love sets us free from all forms of bondage.

Though Christ has died, we must be assured in his resurrection. In John 14:25-27 he said,

“I have said these things to you while I am still with you. But the Advocate, the Holy Spirit, whom the Father will send in my name, will teach you everything, and remind you of all that I have said to you. Peace I leave with you; my peace I give to you. I do not give to you as the world gives. Do not let your hearts be troubled, and do not let them be afraid”.

At Easter we celebrate a memorial of the resurrected Christ, we must recognise the love of God and the sacrifice of Christ who not only suffered humiliation and rejection but a horrible death for the sake of our freedom.

It was after his resurrection that he appeared to his disciples and said to them “All authority in heaven and on earth has been given to me. Go therefore and make disciples of all nations, baptizing them in the name of the Father and of the Son and of the Holy Spirit” Matthew 28:18-19.

The House Of Rainbow Fellowship is extremely important in the understanding that there is room for everyone including LGBTI people and we can celebrate an Easter for Gays.

Rev Father Jide Macaulay

Always Remembered

Ruth Ellis was born in Springfield, Illinois on 23 July 1899, to Charlie Ellis and Carrie Farro Ellis and was the youngest of four children. Her parents were born in the last years of slavery in Tennessee.

Ruth came out as a lesbian around 1915 and graduated from Springfield High School in 1919, at a time when fewer than seven percent of African Americans graduated from secondary school.

In the 1920s, she met the only woman she ever lived with, Ceciline "Babe" Franklin and moved together to Detroit, Michigan in 1937 where Ellis became the first American woman to own a printing business in that city. She made a living printing stationery, fliers, and posters out of her house.

Ellis and Franklin's house was also known in the African American community as the "gay spot". It was a central location for gay and lesbian parties, and also served as a refuge for African American gays and lesbians. Although Ellis and Franklin eventually separated, they were together for more than 30 years.

Ruth's exceptional longevity ran a long course of events that were no less exceptional. She was among the few black women of her generation to obtain a high school education and her father was never a lesbophobe:

"[He] always let me have girlfriends. My lesbianism reassured him. He had a way of saying that boys and books do not make for a good match."

Throughout her life, Ruth was an advocate for the rights of gays and lesbians, as well as for the rights of African Americans.

Affected by the loss of Babe, who died at the beginning of the 1970's, Ruth nevertheless started a new life as she approached 80 years. She became an advocate in the U.S. lesbian/gay community, and in particular for lesbians of colour researching their history and their roots, took some courses in self-defense, made some new friends, including Jaye Spiro [a lesbian self-defense teacher], who was among the first white friends in her growing community.

She went out to the bars, attended concerts, made a tour of lesbian events and among the participants at the annual Michigan Women's Music Festival in August 1999, thousands of women got to see her celebrating her 100th year, dancing on the night stage; hundreds attended the showing of her film, ***Living With Pride: Ruth Ellis @ 100***, which retraces her life and history and is told in conjunction with some US history as well.

Two months before her passing, she travelled again, participating in conferences, and never ceasing to give messages of optimism and of hope.

Ellis became a role model, a figure at the forefront of black, lesbian, and senior pride and, directly or indirectly, the source at the root of several projects for support to seniors, as well as to the African American, gay and lesbian communities.

The Ruth Ellis Center, for example, is a space for shelter and aid for gay/ lesbian/ bisexual / transgendered youth who have run away or are without shelter. She died on 5 October 2000.

Greg Leonard

Eddie Okada-Horsley

Always Remembered

Rudolf Brazda, the last surviving victim of persecution towards homosexuals during WW2, died at the age of 98 years in August 2011. He was sent to Buchenwald concentration camp due to his sexuality: that was his crime.

Brazda was believed to have been the last surviving person sent to a Nazi concentration camp due to his sexuality and was sent there in August 1942, being held there until his release by US forces in 1945.

In those days Nazi Germany declared homosexuality an aberration that threatened the German race and convicted approximately 50,000 homosexuals as criminals – an estimated 10,000 to 15,000 gay men were deported to concentration where very few survived.

Brazda was born in 1913 and grew up in the eastern German town of Meuselwitz where he repeated ran in to trouble with Nazi German authorities over his sexuality before being sent to Buchenwald. On his release he moved and lived in the Alsace region of eastern France and was name a knight in the country's Legion of Honor.

thanks to The Huffington Post

Daniel Sheils

Eve Poland

Wiccan Wonderland

The Wiccan faith has existed for thousands of years and predates Christianity. It is founded upon the main principles of connecting with nature and equality for all, with the general principles of Wiccan beliefs being such that Wicca is an almost completely decentralised religion.

George Knowles, a Wiccan author, has said: **"Wicca has no high authority, no single leader, no prophet and no Bible to dictate its laws and beliefs".**

Most Wiccans are people who practice on their own. Others form small local groups called covens, groves etc. Thus, there probably are almost as many sets of Wiccan beliefs as there are Wiccans. Three if the key principles that most adhere to are:

- principle 2 – this stresses the importance of caring for the environment;
- principle 4 – which affirms the equality of women and men;
- principle 10 – which refers to the intense opposition and oppression experience by many Wiccans, typically from very ultra conservative Christians and others.

In all there are 13 main principles within the Wiccan belief system.

One of the other Wiccan beliefs regards the thousands of ancient Gods and Goddesses including: Athena, Brigit, Diana, Fergus, Odin, Pan and Zeus.

The term 'Wicca' normally implies that the person's religion / belief is based upon Celtic spiritual concepts, its pantheon of deities and seasonal days of celebration.

It must also be stressed that Wiccans have no belief in the supernatural beings that are often found in many other God-based faiths / religions.

It is unfortunate that in one particular branch of the Wicca faith, the Dianic Wicca, transgender people are not allowed – because they are not now the gender in which they were born. This may be viewed as double standards and one in which, although I believe in the Wiccan faith, find hard to associate.

That is also why I often shy away from 'organised faiths' and take aspects of the Wicca faith which resonate more fully with me.

One of the main holidays within the Wicca faith is The Winter Solstice (Yule Lore). Mainly taking place between 20 and 23 December it is called the Winter Solstice in the northern hemisphere and the Summer Solstice in the southern hemisphere.

Symbols of Yule include a 'yule log' or small log with 3 candles, evergreen boughs or wreaths, holly, mistletoe hung in doorways, gold pillar candles, baskets of clove studded fruit and more – including thistle, frankincense etc – don't these symbols sound something that is incorporating and used by other faiths?

Most of which are now part of the Christian calendar and holiday of 'Christmas'.

Despite some of the negative connotations and the discriminatory aspect of one branch of the Wiccan faith, I am a Wiccan because it allows me to be who I am and give back to nature.

I am a Wiccan because it allows me to enjoy my sexuality without feeling that I am no longer 'natural' or 'part of nature'.

anonymous

Glenn Bayes

Thank you to the following for their support, time, effort, images and stories allowing for the completion of ***Through the Eyes of Others***.

Adam Lowe – www.adam-lowe.com
Alain Magallon
Alison Baskerville – www.alisonbaskerville.com
Bari Goddard – www.GoD-photography.co.uk
Charlotte Adejayan - www.facebook.com/pages/Charlotte-Adejayan-Photography/216525525065085
Colette Dathorne
Dan Sheils - www.facebook.com/SheilsPhotography?ref=hl#
David Miles
Eddie Okada-Horsley
Ellis Collins – www.ellis-collins.co.uk
Eve Poland – www.evepoland.com
Glenn Bayes
Hellz Bellz
Julia Czastka
Joe Tedesco
Joel Cable – www.joelcable.com
Kim Hines – www.simplykimhines.com
Nicolas Collins
Nicolas Chinardet – www.zefrog.eu
Murad – www.somaligaycommunity.org
Patricia Nelson – www.kimhinescoach.com
Rev Father Jide Macaulay – www.houseofrainbow.org.uk
Richard Hoey – www.richardhoey.co.uk
Sina Sparrow – www.boycrazyboy.com
Sue Sanders – www.lgbthistorymonth.org
Terry Fenwick – www.schools-out.org.uk
Victoria Candos
XXXora – www.xxxora.com
Zynab Yaseen

raising funds and awareness for

LGBT History Month / Schools OUT UK
www.lgbthistorymonth.org.uk
www.schools-out.org.uk

Royal National Lifeboat Institution
www.rnli.org.uk

The Royal British Legion
www.britishlegion.org.uk

Profits from the sale of this book will be donated to LGBT History Month / Schools OUT UK (35%), The Royal National Lifeboat Institution (20%) and The Royal British Legion (10%).

The remaining 35% will be donated to various other charities, groups and organisations recommended by contributors, including 5% each to:

Educate and Celebrate: www.ellybarnes.com
Inclusion for All: www.inclusionforall.co.uk

Through the Eyes of Others is proud to raises awareness for these charities and groups:

Bowel Cancer UK
www.bowelcanceruk.org.uk
Downs Syndrome Association
www.downs-syndrome.org.uk
Galva108
www.galva108.org
Her Majesty's Prison Memorial Fund
www.hmpmf.co.uk
House of Rainbow
www.houseofrainbow.org
Kings Cross Steelers Rugby Football Club
www.kxsrfc.com
Macmillan Cancer Support
www.macmillan.org.uk
People's Dispensary for Sick Animals
www.pdsa.org.uk
Safra Project
www.safraproject.org
Sahir House
www.sahir.uk.com
Soka Gakkai International
www.sgi.org
The Sussex Beacon
www.sussexbeacon.org.uk
Whizz Kidz
www.whizz-kidz.org.uk
Zardozi
www.afghanartisans.com/test/about_us_test.html